To my beautiful cousin, your memory will live on
as this tree blossoms and grows.

God gained an angel on July 25, 2024

I love you….

Chundrea Johnson

THE GIRL WHO *Fell in Love* WITH DISRESPECT

SHENIECE KAUFFMAN

Chapter 1

Then comes baby

Months before my dad would be released from prison, I had the worst welcome home news that any father would want to hear from their Babygirl." I'm having a baby!" Of course, I knew it tore my parents into pieces, but only my God knew the things that were going on in my head. The only words I had to go off were "In order for the baby to survive you have to." So, I did! I am Here!

As time went by and we began to embrace the fact that my father was home we also began to accept the fact that I was about to become a mom at only eighteen years old. Boy, did I not know I hurt my mom with this one after all her hard work as a single mom trying to push me and my oldest sister through school, which was never an easy task to do.

What I never understood was how a mother could still love her child after being let down so many times like my mother, but she did and never left.

But I ignored my thoughts for a moment and enjoyed life as a child for as long as I could while wishing I would have never tried to go and find love in all the wrong places, especially now that my dad had come home and was turning his life around. Of course, it was too late for that, so I had no choice but to face it head on like the woman I thought I wanted to be. Not for once thinking it would lead me to being pregnant at only 17. Now here I am at the age of eighteen, having my first son.

I lost it...I assumed my life was done, scariest shit a girl could take on. But I did it. Not thinking I had taken on the responsibility of loving and caring for an innocent soul when I was not even capable of loving myself at the time. I still Thank God for some of my family.

After nine whole months of being told my unborn would have some disabilities due to chromosomes not connecting in his brain, I lost it, thinking "I cannot do this!" As time went by it was time for me to have my baby boy. I felt dead but alive enough for me to have this baby.

I remember like yesterday getting rolled into Houston Methodist Hospital weeping like no other, heart pounding, legs trembling from fear that I was about to be a single mom at eighteen. Unfortunately, I experienced postpartum soon after my 9lbs'10 ounce baby had entered the world on January 20, 2003. I must say with all the nurses and support from some of my family and friends I felt a little at ease, I guess it was safe to say the devil did not like that. Soon after being released to go home, the day of my roller coaster ride began and has not stopped since. At the time of having my son I did not know God and did not think I was worthy enough to know him all I knew is I cannot raise this baby because I do not know how but God knew what kind of parents I needed for sure. Finally, I made it home and as I walked up the dark stairways (well at least that's what it felt like to me.) I sat on the edge of my bed in pain slowly trying not to bust the stitches from my c-section open, patiently waiting for my son dead beat dad to enter my room with our three-day old son knowing it would be the last time he would be in the presence of his son, of course it was by his choice.

As soon as my mom went to walk him out of the house and locked the door, the sound of the door locking was like a click from my seatbelt as if the devil had just finished readjusting it a little tighter to make sure I would not fall off this rollercoaster ride, as bad as I wanted to. I still remember it like yesterday as my mom walked back into the room standing there speechless looking at me bawl my eyes out in so much pain, fear, and anger. All I could hear over my loud cry was "Pray Sheniece! Pray!" As her prayer followed right behind it, but because I did not know how to pray, I continued weeping. All I knew is I could not love this beautiful baby boy the way he deserved to be loved.

After a few hours of crying in my sun lighted room staring at my beautiful son thinking the worst thoughts a mother could have, again my mother steps in and says, "I am about to call your God Parents to see if they can take baby boy for a little while until you pull yourself together." But instead, my sister did. I will never forget the next day on a Friday evening my God parents came, and my son went, As I sat there embarrassed but relieved knowing my son was going to be loved properly.

They were gracefully picked to be my God Parents for a reason and on that day, it showed because they had saved my life literally. As months passed and I matured more feeling like I was a woman since I just had a whole baby! I started looking for a man thinking "I am about to see what it is like to be loved by one so I can love my baby boy the same". Boy was I crazy for thinking some shit like that. Soon after my search I had found me a boyfriend, one that was kind, attractive, respectable, loving, and one to bring home to my parents. Most of all he respected my situation with my son.

After almost two years of dating and falling in love with the way he loved me, I was ready to give my son the same kind of love since I knew I could love someone so genuinely. So, I moved to Pearland for some time just to see how I could handle loving my beautiful two- year-old with the guidance of my God parents for a few months, then that day came, and I was ready to try and become the best mother I could be along with my new boyfriend support. Over a brief period, I lost focus on my relationship because motherhood was no joke, I tell you. So now my new boyfriend who was slowly becoming my old boyfriend was not fully capable of loving another man's baby, and I understood that, but what I didn't understand was how am I about to do this mommy thing without my now ex-boyfriend who showed me what a little love felt like. Now that I've already fell in love with my baby boy there was no turning back.

(Prayer For Strength)
Help me not to fear the future but to boldly trust that you control when

my emotions plunge me down, and when I am in despair. And times when I cannot talk and do not know what to say help me to "Be still and know that you are God." Be my comforter, healer and bring me peace. In Jesus name, Amen.

Chapter 2

Looking for a man

"Rise and shine, get up and see you might have to pee!" Saying my mom as she walked in my room to wake me up to tell me I need to go apply for benefits to get some help for my son needs until I find me a job that will take care of the both of us. Scared OUT OF MY MIND to go in this building to get help for my son at twenty years old thinking "I am supposed to be out having fun with my friend's enjoying life. Soon I learned what being a mom meant which was my needs were no longer first. So, I began to train myself to get up and make everyday count as tired as I was from the night before from staying up trying to calm my gassy baby boy.

On that particular day I woke up with a little umph in me, while getting baby boy together to drop him off at daycare in my two door chevy cavalier so I could go and get some things done. After dropping him off I energetically drove to my appointment at the workforce, but before I made it to my destination, I had to pull over for fuel first.

With my music blasting I get out of the car and strutted into the gas station to pay for my gas, but before I make it to the door to enter the store, I hear a strong toned voice say "Say little mama in the red car!" of course I thought in my head "someone really want me?" So as vulnerable as I was, I turned around waiting for him to walk up to me and say something I wanted to hear and reassure him he did. With that strong toned voice, he says, "you gone be my woman." All I wanted to hear!

After our three-minute conversation I had his number and he had mine, meanwhile I was ignoring the fact that he was one of the well- known dope dealers on the block. We finally talked on the phone connecting like no other, he was a little older than me and I could tell by the way he talked to me, including the way he loved his son, which drew me in closer, me thinking he had qualities in loving my 2-year-old son just off of his experience and if I did not get nothing else out of it, he would at least teach me how to love in a more confident way.

A few months went by, and we are all in love, so I was ready to do everything he asked me to do like moving in together, of course I jumped on it just to be out of my parents' house to raise my son with the help of my new man.

The next morning, I woke up to a song by Jahiem called "Never" playing loud as crap which was the sound of my phone blowing up that morning. Soon as I answer I hear "what's up? I thought we had to pick up the key today? As I am replying my son is now waking up saying Eat! Eat! So, my day had officially began at 9am on a Saturday morning. As I pulled in the motel to pick him up, I'm hesitantly getting out of my car to get in the passenger seat to let him take over the wheel. Meanwhile, I am sitting there sneaking looking for the blue car I met him in, but it was nowhere in sight. Now, here my mind is all over the place and heart racing thinking am I sure I want to pick this key up to this apartment that had only my name on it with no job or nothing. Silly me walked right into the leasing office with the most confusing look on my face and signed that damn lease.

So here we go in our new apartment all lovey Dovey, I remind you that I'm now a stay home mom at only twenty years old going on twenty-one with no work history to save my life. Meanwhile, I had him in my ear reassuring me that he is going to take care of me and my baby boy. For a minute I thought I had the best life. All I had to do was wake up to him and my son, clean the house, and wash his clothes when needed, cooking was close to never because he made sure he kept me fed with my favorite wings from a spot he had made me fall in love with from all the times he took me when he wanted me to forgive him for all the wrong he had done. Now, I cannot stand that place. As a few months close to a year had passed and I was now twenty-one and feeling like I was ready to do something different, something that a mother should always do and that was go to work and provide. I literally had no clue as to what I needed to do, so of course since he had taught me how to take care of him so well, I just knew he could tell me the steps of taking care of myself. Now being that my man had to work all night and sometimes never come home I had to make sure I caught him at the right time before the streets called him again, and I finally did at four in the morning.

As I laid on the couch drowning in my tears from not getting my calls answered for six hours straight this man had the nerve to walk in the house and ask me "why are you not in bed my homeboy is about to come in?" Boy! If looks could kill, he would have been dead. I finally got up and went to bed with my mind racing my heart pounding in fear and anger thinking what have I done? An hour later goes by an he walks in the room, and I shout out "I am going to look for a job in the morning, so I am going to need my own car!" He responds back saying "I will take you to Walmart and help you fill out the job application." Just what I needed him to say because I had no idea of what to do. I was so relieved that he offered to help me, I had forgotten about everything that had happened that day and soon found myself apologizing for something he had done to me. Being who I was I just wanted to make it right and not argue or wake baby boy up who was sleeping so peacefully right next to me.

Not to mention the kiss on my forehead before wrapping his strong arms around me putting me fast to sleep. Not knowing he was just comforting me before the worst part. The next morning come with my loud alarm I had set to wake me up to get baby boy to daycare early so me and my man could go fill out my first application. We walked straight to the kiosk and finish the application in about one hour walking out knowing I had the job just because he assured me, he knew what he was doing and since I trusted him just as much as I believed in him, I had no doubt the job was mine. Guess where he took me when we left? The wing spot! Just to set the tone for the ride we were about to go on right after since he made it clear he had to make a stop after we leave the restaurant.

Absolutely I agreed to it as if I had another choice. As we are riding, I notice the navy-blue car I had met him in at the gas station pull in the store parking lot right behind us with another woman driving it, while he sat in the driver's seat looking stupid and nervous as he pulled to the side putting the car in park he reaches in his pocket and pulls out a bag of drugs and roll my window down and hand it to the customer standing there if you get my drift. Acting as if he wasn't bothered by the car that pulled up right behind us. As the man walk off, I am sitting there in the passenger seat of my car livid only for the bastard to say, "Do not get out of the car I will be right back." without a response from me he gets his short ass out of the car and attempt to approach the blue car I had met him in, but before he makes it to the car the girl meets him halfway shouting "who are you with?" of course I'm about to go deaf and blind trying to see and hear what is actually going on and who else could it have been other than the mother of his son. I only assumed that as I hear him saying "Where is my son?" and "Who's watching over him?" As she walks in the store that we were parked in front of to go to work. Meanwhile, I turned back around in my seat crying and confused, caring less about what happened next. After a few minutes goes he gets back in the car driving off looking through the mirror making sure we were not being followed by the mother of his child or maybe even the police since he had made a drug deal before he had approached his ex. I was scared and angry at the same time, so I just stayed silent, which scared him even more. I knew that because his slow ass had taken me to my favorite wing spot place, he had just taken me to a few hours before all the madness. I think in his mind that wing spot had become my happy place and safe to say I made the bastard feel that way because every time

I walked out of those doors I was full and happy all over again. It was like a room that cleared all the bad he was doing to me. I only say that because soon after we left, I had forgotten the fact that he was just put out by the mother of his child. So, it's safe to say that I had turned into a rebound chick and had not even known it until that day after I done moved in with this man and fell quickly in love with the devil. It was somewhere close to 6pm meaning it was time to get baby boy from daycare. Now I'm back into mommy mode as I walked into the daycare to get my son putting everything that had happened that day into the back of my head. As, months go by my feelings grew stronger for all his toxic love that he had to give I knew I had fallen in love with the devil an I thought it felt so good at the time because I didn't know any better and I think at some point he knew that and used it against me in every way that he knew how. Especially after I stop complaining about him being out all night in my car to do lord knows what. Little did he know I was just getting tired and close to my breaking point everything in me was screaming "LEAVE!" After getting into rotation of taking my son to daycare and working from 2pm-11pm Monday thru Friday while he is out doing whatever the fuck he wants. I started making my own money consistently and began to feel like I could do it alone without dealing with all the disrespect and toxicity that he came with. The next day came, and it was an off day for me, so I take my son to daycare and back home to get back in bed with my man hoping the day goes better than the days before. As I walked back into the house his friend was sitting on the couch waiting for him to get dressed to go on with their normal routine and that was the last straw for me, I had had enough of everything. First words that had come out of my mouth when we made eye contact was

"Get Out!" Why would I say that to a man who had nowhere to go? Before I knew it, he was towards me, and we were connecting like never before in the most physical way a young girl like me would have even imagine. After that moment I knew I had made the worst decision ever just to be loved, and the relationship had to end so we both agreed to move out and go our separate ways. But never completely cutting ties. Soon after I moved back home with my parents, and he went wherever he wanted, which wasn't a good idea because weeks later he was locked up and best believe little old me stayed in position just like he knew I would. Finally, the time had come for him to be released 2 years later. Only difference was he had to parole to his mom house which I thought was a good thing because I would know where he would be but, one thing a sister learned was whatever a man wanted to do he would most definitely make it happen and I mean that in the worst way. As time went by and women came and went as we took turns unknowingly visiting him at his mom home until the day, he was free from it all and that was including me. He was like a loose chicken with his head cut off. I began being cheated on, lied to, disrespected, and everything else a young girl feared, but I stayed and took it all because he made me feel like I was strong enough to handle it. Until one day a close friend called me and said, "I have something to tell you that's going to hurt you!" But in my mind, I felt I could handle whatever it was since I've taken everything else like a champ. Not knowing that she was about to tell me clearly cheating with a whore who was a stranger to me, wasn't enough for him he needed to do more damage and that he did. I had enough but unfortunately the devil hadn't.... My God, my rock, in whom I take refuge, my shield, and the horn of my salvation, my stronghold and my refuge, my savior you save me from violence. I call upon the Lord, who is worthy to be praised, and I am saved from my enemies. Samuel 22: 3-4

Chapter 3

Learning Lesson

I was having another baby by yet another man who disrespected me 5 years later. In my mind the roller coaster had yet to stop to let me off, it had only sped up. Now here I am back in my parents' home with nowhere to run with not only one baby but another one on the way. At this point I was numb because I knew better but I just wanted to feel loved and if ignoring all the bad just to see the good in this man was all I had to do I was willing to "Dumbest shit ever I know." Now that it was over it was time to heal from the heartbreak and be strong for my innocent babies. After going through 9 long miserable months of going to every doctor visit, baby registry, and baby shower all alone it was now time to do the same thing in the delivery process, this time I was better because I already went through it once so the second time was a charm, so at this point I was just ready to meet baby girl. But what I came to the realization of is that I needed nobody but Jesus and in my parents' home is where I needed to be to gain some help finding him. And months later I did. I began to pray for understanding the best way I knew how since praying had become so foreign to me and what he brought to me shortly after the prayers became so consistently is that "I have to put him first in all that I do!" So, I began to try it. Now what I did not know is the devil will work harder on intervening while trying to lean on God for understanding. Reason being is the devil saw my weakness which was looking for love in a man instead of the lord. So, while getting in my car the next morning to go get baby girl milk and cereal my guy friend from years before pulls up to the end of my parents drive way getting out of his car immediately expressing how he had been looking for me for so long and how much he was ready to settle down and make me his wife. Everything a girl wants to hear at Twenty- Eight right? So, me thinking I'm doing everything right by only dating him for a year taking things slowly so that I could see his dark side if he had one but, I'll tell you one thing "a man can hide his dark side until you have given him your mind body and soul." After all of our dates, parties, meetings of his daughters, and him telling me he loves me. I decided we should take it to the next step, and that was by moving in together and I felt safe enough to do that only because he constantly told me how much he hates being away from me. Whew! A man that makes you feel wanted is everything right? Yeah, only if it's coming from a genuine place in his heart and not because he sees the weakness and kindness you have in yours. So, I felt like now I can do something positive which was began my career since my then man was talking marriage, I needed to have my duckies in a row. Before we moved in three months later, I was enrolled in beauty school and doing hair on the side to still provide for myself and the now two kids that I am raising all by myself. I forgot to mention he was also a street man shall I say, and yes, he was promising to take care of all the bills as long as I took care of home while going to school. Of course, that was like putting icing on a cake since I had just done the same thing a few years before. So, as time went by and he saw me becoming more popular with my clients and the guys from school being all over me, his jealousy and dark side began to show slowly but surely. One evening I come home from picking up my kids from the daycare and making groceries ready to cook his favorite meal but before I even get a chance to get started, he greets me at the door saying in his deep dry voice "I'm going to Miami in the morning for some business." Knowing he wanted me to act out but, instead I did the exact opposite, I held it together while dying inside thinking "I did it yet again!" Allowed yet another man take full advantage of me. The next morning came, and he was gone for his flight at six in the morning, I still remember like yesterday how I sat on the patio crying from sunup to sundown hiding so my kids would not see me at my worst. Now what killed me was even though I knew he was going to be with another woman I stayed in position waiting for his return hoping my insecurities were all wrong. So, for the three days he was gone I stayed focused on my kids, school, and home the best I could when I was not on the patio bawling my eyes out.

Now, Monday comes and the kids are at school and I'm at home on the couch waiting for him to walk through the door since I had not talked to him in three long days, talking about a sister anxiety on One Hundred! Finally, there is the knock I have been waiting for as I open the door, he greets me with a wet forehead kiss and walks in the room put his bags down and jumps right in the shower he goes. At this point I began to call on God for the first time in a long time because I knew exactly why he jumped in the shower so fast, and I was indeed about to react. As I waited for him to come out of the restroom I went through his bags and "My God!" is the first thing that came out of my mouth. I saw numerous of his clothing with make-up, lipstick, and the most disgusting semen all over his basketball shorts. Soon after the bathroom door open and he walks out and go in the kitchen to get his tray to roll a special cigarette if you get my drift, I politely walk over and showed him the make-up, lipstick, and semen on his clothing he looks up with a smirk on his face and say, "Don't question me!" Before he could finish the sentence, I had slung the tray off the kitchen counter and shortly after he had me by my neck with my feet off the ground and grasping for air. All I heard him saying once he let me go and my body hit the floor was "I'm Sorry." While down there trying to get my breathe and strength back all I kept thinking was "I am too weak to stand on my own." not realizing God was trying to get my attention and I kept on ignoring him. Time went by and my body had healed, I had forgiven him. The disrespect cycle was still going on. Weeks later he went to the strip club and didn't come home until the next day and that was all I was willing to take. Clearly, he was disrespecting me on purpose so as a mother of two I had to do what was best for my kids and that was to leave. And I Did!

The Lord delights in those who fear him, who put their hope in his unfailing love." "There is surely a future hope for you, and your hope will not be cut " off." "Therefore my heart is glad and my tongue rejoices; my body also will rest secure."

Psalms 147:11-12

Chapter 4

Trying to break the cycle

Now, as a few months have gone by and I've been holding it together from being back at my parents' home trying to figure out where did I go wrong these past years with these men I chose, the only thing that came to mind was that God wanted my attention! But what scared me the most was I did not know if I had the capability to focus long enough to give him my undivided attention because I had so many distractions around me including this young man who had just moved across the street from my parents' home into his mom home. Little did I know my life was about to change forever. One evening me and my mom were pulling up from the grocery store, as we got out the car to get the groceries out, the guy from across the street was pulling up to his mom house, of course I'm trying not to make eye contact but me being me (nosey) I did! But before I could look away, he waves his hand to speak to me and my mom, I continued walking to the door to take the groceries in while thinking of a reason to go sit outside to watch him throw the football with his younger brother with his sweatpants and muscle shirt on.

Whew! Guess what? I rolled me a joint and went to my parents' garage and enjoyed the show as I talked with my best friend at the time. My friend was talking, and I was so focused on him I didn't hear a thing she had said all I remembered her saying was "Girl what the hell are you doing?" as I replied saying "Girl let me call you back he's walking over here!" Not knowing that would be me and her last conversation for a while. As he approaches me with his New Orleans accent asking me what's my name? And I'm already giving him my number right behind it. Gullible me I know. And best believe I quickly assumed he would be different since he wasn't from Houston. Wasn't that the dumbest shit I could have thought of. What I didn't know is he was about to make my next few years a rollercoaster ride I would never forget! That first phone call was everything I wanted in a man, someone who would listen to me express myself and what I wanted while he continuously calls me his sweet strawberry until we fell asleep but the best part of it all at the time was, I got to wake up the next morning to him softly breathing in the phone. Thinking oh yeah, I could get use to this. Not realizing until we hung up the phone that I just told this boy I barely even know everything I wanted in a man now thinking he was going to do all of what I wanted until he got tired, but I went for it anyway. A few days went by, and we went from talking on the phone all day to sitting in my parents driveway for hours in my new car I had just bought. One particeular night I decided to ask him why is he single and he began to sweat before he even began to tell me, it went something like this. As, the tears rolled down his eyes before he began to say "I just got out of a bad relationship." That was my first red flag that I ignored. As I Proceeded to ask why was it messed up? Feeling like I'm a counselor and shit. He continued by saying his ex-played him into thinking the child she was pregnant with was his and she wouldn't tell him where the baby was, he continued on to say she had come over one day and told him the baby was in the system which caused him to pin her down with his knee on her neck out of frustration. I can't lie I was confused on should I run and never look back or do I stay and try to help him heal? Guess what my weak ass did? Stayed and tried to help him heal and love him pass his pain. Meanwhile, I'm wiping his tears that wasn't from hurt but from laughing at me on the inside because I was actually falling for it. As he goes on to tell me about his 5-year-old son that he has with another woman who won't let him see his son while going through a court battle. My emotional ass sat back in that driver's seat and soaked it all in thinking these two women before me just didn't see the good in this man. He literally got in my head just how he had planned to. From that night forward we began to connect from all the lies he told and the love I immediately began to show him. He knew from what I told him when we first met the kind of man I wanted, things I expected, and what I endured before him, promising He is nothing like that. As time went by three months to be exact, I thought I was safe thinking I can give him the special part of me. Boy! Wasn't I wrong for thinking something like that! The three months I held out was just giving the devil enough time to lengthen that rollercoaster ride. So, as we continue to love on one another we learned a few things that should had been discuss at the friendship stage that we never really even went through, which was what our beliefs were. One day we had a situation where I needed God to step in so I asked did he believe in God because I felt we needed to pray together. Because I truly believe in the saying "Where two or three gather in my name, there am

I with them." But because he didn't believe in God, it left me standing there looking really stupid and empty on the inside so I had to stand there and look at him in his eyes hoping that the prayer I'm saying in my head is connecting and entering his spirits through our eyes. Let me be the first to tell you it did not. As a short time went by, I began to find myself praying less I became so focused on him and our relationship to the point to where I had lost not only myself but my God too. The moment I realized I had lost my connection with God I slowly began to lose everything else. I became pregnant with our first child a year in, I lost the baby. I had a brand-new car when I got with him, I lost that, my current job I prayed so hard for after my previous relationship, I lost that. I never understood that then because all I knew was, I was deeply in love with a boy that I didn't want to lose so I was willing to lose everything except him. While he was not caring if I came or went.

"But God showed his great love for me, while sending Christ to me while I was still a sinner."

Romans 5:8

Chapter 5

Soul Ties

I didn't understand what soul ties were until after all of the things I had to go through in this relationship. In case it's not a familiar word or you've never experienced or have experienced and just did not know what was going on let me help you understand. It is where a connection with someone deeply embedded in your soul. Now, there is a Godly and an Ungodly soul tie which is clearly what I had going on which is having sex outside of marriage in physical affection with the intent, or thought, of having sex outside of marriage. Now here we are Seven months in and I'm now pregnant again by him after the doctors told me not to try for another year or so, but silly me did just that. This time I found some time to talk to God and ask him to strengthen my body to carry this baby for nine months. Oh! And he did! But the lesson he was trying to teach me was not a easy one, he made sure I got what I wanted and learn a lesson at the same time. So once we agreed on bringing this baby into the world right after the control, disrespect, cheating, abuse, manipulation, belittling, and everything else a woman would fear. Not to leave out we were already in the midst of moving in together before finding out about my now third child. A month later him, myself, and my two innocent children moved into our happy place. Not knowing we were moving from heaven to hell. I found myself repeating the same cycles of cooking, cleaning, washing clothes, and making sure I wasn't being cheated on. Expecting nothing back but love and affection, and never received it. Months go by and we are well into our new place, I will never forget. It was hurricane season and almost my birthday may I add. That particular month hurricane Harvey hit us, me thinking I really knew this man I was having a baby by everything was going to be just fine since he went and helped total strangers the first night it touched down, I just knew whatever needed to be done will get done. Fooled myself again. So, after staying at my mom home for a week I was ready to go back home a and make sure our things were ok, I called him before he left work and nicely asked him "can we go home and check on our things when you get off?" He agreed and we ended the conversation. Now, here come seven in the afternoon, he pulls up get out of the car an walk right pass me as if I was a ghost or something, leaving me standing there squeezing myself making sure I was not one myself, then following right behind him as he walked in the room we shared at my mom home until we checked on our own.

Let's just say he sent me alone to check on the apartment we shared together to get our things, let me not forget to mention the apartment had mold everywhere but, I went in anyway and packed my kids' things, mine, and some of his too. Not thinking about my unborn who was due the following month. Now one thing I was unsure about on my ride back to my mom home was should I pray or let the devil dance, thinking selfishly in my mind "He didn't believe in God anyway." so it was a safe zone. Not knowing at the time God was judging me by what I do and not by what this man was doing to me. I didn't know God was already working it out. But because I was running from God I wasn't willing to wait for his work. I walked back in the room with our things and he is knocked out in my old bed I grew up in which upset me even more. I guess that was God way of working it out for him through the night because when morning came, I was ready to turn my gospel on and treat him like a ghost how he did me the day before. Unfortunately, when you are dealing with a man who has control issues your only choice is to talk when spoken to because when you do you will be unheard anyway. After he repeatedly asked me what was wrong with the apartment and could we go back? I finally responded with "If you were concerned you would have been there with me!" But assuming he was wrong all he did was storm out of the room after telling me to shut my dumb ass up. Meanwhile, I'm standing there starring at the back of the door praying asking God to "Let no weapon form against me and my daughter who was there at the time. What I learned in that instance is you have to watch what you ask God for because that devil did not stop dancing. I took a deep breath not knowing that it was about to be a chance that it could be my last one. Walking in the living room behind him as he sits on my mom couch and power the tv on. I politely tell him we need a minute apart because we can't be doing this at my mom house, let's not forgethe would be only going across the street to his mom house but that was not what he wanted to hear. He snatched the remote out of my hand and stood up over me while I am standing there looking up to him as he looks me in my eyes and say "You better go!" I stood there looking confused as ever thinking "But this Is my parents' house. So, as I reach for the remote to the tv before my hand could touch it me and his unborn child flew across the floor into the brick fireplace, as I try to reach for the metal stick laying on the brick, he pulls my legs dragging me from it while the whole time I am faced down squishing the life out of our thirty-six-week unborn baby boy, thinking this man is about to kill me. Seconds later all I remembered was him having his knee on my neck and me laying there now screaming for my life hoping my daughter would not hear me, he finally let up and I found my way up fighting for my life literally, not even two minutes in I was pinned back down hanging off of my mom couch having my life choked out of me and before I blacked out all I heard was my daughter scream "Get off my mommy!" After laying there for a minute with him standing there over me scared out of his mind thinking he had killed me, I jumped up snatched his phone and ran in the room to call the police but by the time I made it in the room my heart had changed that quick and I decided not to call the police on him, and being that he had fled the scene they would have missed him anyway. Now, that he had left it had caused all type of emotions to come back which caused me to blame myself and feel bad that he was gone, so instead of calling the police I was trying to figure out how can I call him being that I was standing there with his phone in my hand. Not for one minute until after my sister, son, mom, and dad had walked in the house did I realize my son had not made a move inside of my womb for a while, forgetting I was even pregnant up unto the point when my sister walked up talking to my belly, I had forgotten I was even carrying a baby due to the way my While she is bent over talking, she feels my wet tear drop man had just fought me. on her hand and look up and ask me "where is he at?" Assuming she saw the scratches and bruises on my neck I began to cry out loud telling them all what had taken place just an hour before. So, one thing about my sister, she is going to react let me just say that first. She grabs her phone and calls 9-1-1 and before they could answer she yells out "get an ambulance and the police here now!" with the 9-1-1 operator asking right behind her request "what is your emergency Ma'am?" then my sister angrily replied "My sister boyfriend fought her and now my nephew has not moved for hours!" Causing me to realized what really just happened one week before my baby shower. Now I am sitting there drowning in my own tears not worrying about what he just did to me but more focused on where was he at and was he ok, thirty minutes went by and we get the hardest bang on the door meanwhile I am sitting there scared not knowing if it was him coming back to finish me off or if it was the police come to arrest him. Best believe it was the police there to arrest him. No! I did not press charges on my man. Thinking that would have made him understand the love I had for him and when I say that didn't help him understand nothing but one thing! And that was how weak I really was and that is all he needed to see. Soon after being released from the hospital from getting checked out me and my unborn, and my sister was on our way back to my mom home. Lost and confused and with hopes that he would call since his mom had come over to get his phone just to check on me or at least his son and yes you guessed it, he never did. The next morning come and I find myself getting up out of my bed feeling empty as I do not know what, all I knew is I had to wake up and face reality of now being a single mother of three. All because I just wanted to be loved by a man by any means necessary. Yes! I was one of those girls who yearned to be loved by a man, I missed a lot of that from my father growing up and all I knew is I wanted that feeling and wasn't going to stop until I got it. Finally, the time had come and I had to do the hardest part which was pack me and my kid's things to move out of our home which was hell in real life, so I get up while again crying for the one hundredth time hoping that he would call before I found my keys and he never did. I could not understand why I could not have enough of this man especially with all the harsh things he had done to me in a short period of time, until I spent a whole day watching videos on YouTube about soul-ties and finally accepted the fact that me and this man have a soul-tie and the only way to break that was by the work of God. And at this point I wasn't ready to let God work in my life because the devil had me and I say that in the most displeasing way but all I knew and felt at the time is I did not want to break this soul-tie!

May God himself, the God of Peace, sanctify you through. May your whole spirit, soul and body be kept blameless at the coming of our Lord Jesus Christ.

1 Thessalonians 5:23

Chapter 6

When Prayer Changes Things

So here me, and my angry fed-up parents and my kids go driving to go get our things out of this molded apartment while he is at work. With my dad going in first making sure it was safe enough for me to go in I followed right behind him seeing that this man had already gotten his things and left. Standing there weak as ever hurt knowing this man wasted no time to leave me and not look back after all the trauma he had caused upon my life. Meanwhile my father standing there shaking his head at me out of frustration because Im still crying over this boy after he just almost caused me my life and his unborn child. But at the time that was not registering in my mind yet, all I know is I need him in my life to raise this baby boy who was coming in less than a month! So putting in some effort I walk into my room and go into my closet and turned the light on seeing none of my things. Knowing in my mind he had done something drastic, but that heart of mine was hoping he had taken them with him into a new place for us to resides in. Right, foolish me I know. So as I continue to walk the apartment to see what else he had taken I walk into the bathroom and see every piece of clothing I owned from my bras, panties, shoes, clothes, and sleep clothes in the bathtub bleached with a big bottle of acetone sitting on top of them as well. I'm sure for a lot of you reading this book would have been gone and done, but for me I was still thinking I should try to still fix it for the sake of our son, not for once thinking it was God trying to tear it apart. So with nothing but my furniture and my kids things to take we were now headed back to the storage place he worked at hoping he was not there. Finally, back at my mom home trying to figure out if I'm dreaming or is this really taking place. Until I called him an he answers and say "we need time apart." as I respond with why? He hangs up I'm sure he was with another woman and now knowing whenever he is done with her, he can come back to me without a struggle and yes, I knowingly made him feel that way. Now I know you are about ready to close the book and throw it away but do not! It's a purpose for the pain so just keep going I'm going to bless you.

Be strong and courageous, do not be afraid or discouraged for the lord your god is with you wherever you go.

Joshua 1:9

Tomorrow is my baby shower and I am in my mom back room bawling my eyes out again for the hundredth time feeling sad, embarrassed, hurt, empty, broken, depressed, suicidal, sorry, confused, worthless, and the list goes on but one thing I was sure of is I was not done trying to keep him in my life. Sending a text asking him will he be showing up to his son baby

So now the time has come for me to put on another smile while dying on the inside knowing he would not be showing up. As, I finally get up dreading getting that day over with I had my best friend at the time busting through my room door with her caboodle filled with make-up ready to glam me up, let's just say she gave me enough glam to get up and get beautiful for my special day with hopes he would walk in to the baby shower and admire me for once because I was never really a make-up girl my natural beauty was always my choice until I had met this boy.

September 9,2017 the day of my baby shower was here and I was at a place of wishing I never would have woken up that day, filled with shame, anger, bitterness, hurt, and let's not forget a whole lot of soreness from the fight me and my unborn son father and I had just had almost a week before. Walking in this baby shower seeing so many people who came to support me at such a devastating time was what I needed at that moment, but all I could think about was the one person I needed the most at the time was not here with me and the moment I realized that I knew it would be a matter of time before my emotions spilled out. As I walk around greeting my family and friends and some of his as well, I finally get to his mom who walked around like nothing happened glad that I'm holding it together and not exposing what her son had did to me. But what she and I did not know then is that all of it was about to change. The time had come for me to open baby boy gifts, before it happened, I just felt like I had to get the cry out before I sat in front of a crowd of people and pretend that I was ok. Meanwhile, his mom watching every move I make, she sends his sister in the restroom to check on me, but secretly coming in to remind me not to break down and let the cat out the bag. I'm sure you all have heard the old folks tell you that. Walking back out ready to open little man gifts hoping that some type of smile would show up at any point of opening my gifts. You guessed it! Soon as I opened the first gift and sat it in the empty seat where his father should have been sitting it was over, I was ready to go home and bawl up in my bed and cry my eyes out. A day later I get a call from him apologizing for not showing up and of course his only excuse was he didn't want to add fuel to the fire. What he didn't know is what he did cause the fire from the start!

Now we are a few weeks in from having our son and only thing I could be thinking is how do me and this boy fix this relationship before baby boy come in this world, and of course the easiest thing for me to do came to mind so aggressively, which was all I needed, and that was to just take the blame to make it all go away and I did just that! So, here we go trying to figure out how to secretly build our relationship back up, without once thinking about how it would affect the people around us whom knew how toxic our relationship had gotten, like his mom, and both of my parents, Now, unless you have experienced being in an abusive, toxic, manipulating, disrespectful, and last but not least and ungodly soul-tie, you are probably somewhere holding your forehead thinking why won't this woman just leave? Just keep reading I am going to bless you, as my pastor would say. Now just with everything that has been taking place in my life I started to pray, maybe not as much as I should but just enough to get by and let God know how much I needed him for the moment. One thing I did not know then that I very well know now, is that you can not only call on God when everything is going wrong, you still need to praise him even when things are going well, and that I did not do. So, as that one Prayer I prayed after almost a year of us building our relationship God began to open up doors for us, we were finally approved to move in our new apartment in November, God had even blessed with a well-paying job off of my prayers for him, because praying was not a thing in his eyes and that is why everything we tried to build was being torn down in the wink of an eye, and I am also to blame because I stopped praying soon as God had answered all of my prayers as him well. But what that one prayer taught me if nothing else is Prayer Changes Things.

"And all things, whatsoever ye shall ask in Prayer, believing, Ye shall receive."

Matthew 21:22

Chapter 7

The Final Move

So, here we are all moved in our once again new place getting everything all set up not for once thinking about everything that had taken place, but just know God was about to do something that I could not do on my own, and that was tear it apart. So, as things seem to fall in place, I began to pray more and more asking god to keep me focused on him and his word, but what I will say is when the devil is pulling you one way and God is pulling you the other it can be a hard battle and what I want you to know before you even get to the end of my story is that God won that battle! First morning in my new apartment that he moved me in was such a breeze, I woke up with a guy in my living room mounting a big tv on my fireplace, love songs playing, windows open with a cool breeze coming through while I slowly sit on the couch in pain from just being released from the hospital from stressed related issues from everything that had been taking place. Like his mother not showing up to my son first birthday party with his cake, and if any of you are like me, "what is a party without a cake?" but any who I'll hold off on my petty ways this time. Next day come and I am up bright and early to see him off to work at 4am in the morning just so I can kiss him before he leaves knowing he did not care if I kissed him or not but somehow he tricked me and began to kiss me before he got out of bed saving me a broken rest an actually helped me sleep even better after his kiss causing me to get comfortable and put my guards down quickly. The only thing different about this particular move to this new apartment is that I took God with me this time! My kids were enjoying the fact that they now had their own rooms and baby boy was sharing a room with me and his dad, everything seemed so perfect until the devil had enough.

Following week coming and I'm putting in applications like crazy hoping someone call me soon because knowing this man it was a matter of time before the belittling came, in spite of me still feeling like I'm battling with post-partum depression or simply depression since it was over a year that my son had been born, I can count on him to make me feel less than I already did from all the things he had done in the past. One evening he come home and tell me that he was taking our son to his niece birthday party, yes the one who mom or grandmother showed up to my son birthday party, so of course I wasn't having it, not only because they did not show up with a cake for my son birthday party or even apologize about it, but because my sister had already asked to get baby boy that same weekend, but due to the control he thought he still had over me, when I told him that he would not be going because my sister already asked to get him his response was "try to play with me and see what happen son." In his New Orleans accent. So, I walked off giving him no emotion whatsoever leaving him standing there clueless. What he didn't know is I was walking off praying in my head just asking God quickly to just step in an protect me and my kids not knowing what would be next. That night he gets in the bed still cuddling and kissing me like he loved me but really thinking he was changing my mind on sending my son with my sister on the next day, but he wasn't! Laying in the bed eyes wide open and heart empty as ever thinking what if he leaves me and I have to move back home and start over since I had no Job, but my prayer came shortly behind those thoughts, not fully knowing if God was hearing them or not but because I saw God work through my dad life growing up, I knew even if God didn't answer them when I asked, he was stilling hearing them, he was just waiting on me to show him I was able to use the strength that he had given me when I asked him a few months prior. Friday is here and Karter is dressed waiting on 5pm to come so he can greet his aunt who just could not get enough of him, who actually thought she was his mom, but that's a topic for another day. So, while on my way back home from dropping Karter off my oldest son calls me asking "mom what's going on? V just walked in and asked where you were and when I told him you were dropping Karter off he packed some stuff and left." I don't even remember saying bye to my son before hanging up to call him. After getting the voicemail for a hour straight he finally answers saying "you want to show me you going to do what you want so I'm going to show you!" hanging the phone up in my face quickly before I could say anything. Meanwhile sitting in that apartment finding myself in the same place as I was in all the other apartments we had previously moved from. This time instead of crying I prayed asking God "what's next?" I called him all night hoping that he would answer and say he was on his way to me but he never did until four days later and by then I was done! Crazy part is he called to warn me he was coming home to get in his bed like he really cared if I cared or not, but because I wasn't sure of what comes next, I was not letting him in that apartment until I was out. That night he comes banging on the door to get in threatening to call the police on me like he really wanted to be there. After a while he finally realized I wasn't letting him in, he leaves and go back to the woman he had been with for days.

"So do not fear, for I am with you; do not be dismayed, for I am your God. I will strengthen you and help you; I will uphold you with my righteous right hand."

Isaiah 41:10

The next morning come and I wake up to a phone call from one of the job applications I had put in a week prior, asking me can I come in for a interview the next day? Quickly replying with a yes! Soon as I hung up I yelled out "Thank You Jesus!!" and from that point on I realized that all you have to do is ask God and that I began to do often! But the one thing I wasn't fully sure on was how do I trust and believe that what I asked him for he was going to deliver on time. Until things just slowly started to happen, once I got the call from the job my day had begun to start off on the right track, I'm now sitting on the edge of my sofa feeling happy knowing that my new job would be able to get me back on my own two feet again, and on the other hand feeling empty, sorry, sad and last but not least DONE! Knowing that this man did not love me like he said he did and I began to realize and accept it all at once, and quickly got all my things packed and ready to be moved out by my nephew and cousins.

Must I remind you we were only in this apartment for two weeks. As I call the front office to let them know that I will be moving out, before I even got to the point of telling her what my reasonings were and to ask if I would lose the six-hundred-dollar deposit that he paid upon our move in date, the leasing agent was apologizing to me for the plumbing issue we were dealing with since the first day we moved in and told me that she would gladly let me out of my lease and refund me my deposit without putting it on my record as a broken lease. So listen to me when I say this "When God is in the midst you will not be Missed!" And that was the first time in my life that I had Physically felt God in the midst of my trouble. And I can truly say that I found God in the place where I thought I had lost him. Keep reading I am going to bless you.

And lead us not into temptation, but deliver us from the evil one."

Matthew 6:13

Chapter 8

Nobody Like Jesus

So now that I'm back at my mom home in the same place I ended back at each time a relationship had failed. The only thing different about this time is I had God with me, so as I began to go through the whole heartbreak process this particular one was the most difficult one, I had ever experienced, especially because I was old enough to understand everything like knowing my worth and who I was as a woman. But like I said before God is the only one who has the power to break a soul-tie so that is where most of my time had to go! Don't think for one moment that the devil has disappeared. A month later I get a call saying, can you meet me at the park so we can talk? A part of me wanted to hang up the phone and another part wanted to hear what he had to say knowing it was part of whatever plan he had hidden in his cold heart. And I know that from the very first conversation that he and I had. We both pull up to the park, he gets out the car with a evil grin while I'm walking up emotionally drained looking ran down while I'm sure was what he came to see. First words out of his mouth was "damn you lost weight" and with no response back I just looked down at myself eyes filled with tears waiting on him to finish telling me how bad I look, shortly after he finished saying a bunch of nothing I left, driving back to my mom house praying asking God in that instance to just keep building me up. What I want you women to know is do not ever let a man make you feel that you deserve anything less than their best, and if their best make YOU still feel less, then put that mess to rest! God will not bless no mess!

So, this is now the part of my story where God had to change me, and how the holy spirit came in off just one prayer that I wrote down the day after I met him at the Park and it went something like this.....

Heavenly father, I come to you today with a broken heart and a clouded mind, asking that you change my mind and my heart, help me to become a better mother, daughter, sister, friend, and last but not least a child of God, and while you do it help me to trust you in the process, let no weapon form against me and my family. I asked with a pure heart that you would just bring me back to you and break every chain that has a hold of me, give me my strength back! In Jesus name I Pray! Amen!

So here I am starting my first day at my new Job, not even listening to what my trainer was explaining to me about what my position consisted of, mind full of crazy thoughts and flashbacks of the things that this man had intentionally took me through. But while that thought was clouding my mind something even more powerful followed behind it and that was God letting me know that I did not lose anything, I was actually gaining back what I thought I had lost, which was my income, which was two dollars more than what I was making a few months ago, my strength, my faith, my passion to love myself again, and when I say that was the hardest part of it all, because I had let this man for six years make me feel like I was nothing but the ground he walked on. Now knowing this healing process was going to be nothing nice, I literally had nothing left but my kids and the little faith that I was still hanging on to, especially since I just witnessed God make a way out of no way! But, because I didn't understand the bible everything was a blur, so I felt like I had to figure it out the best way I could. The one thing I now believe that I never believed in my life, is that spirits are real! The man that I had been with for years had left me with a spirit that had caused me to be scared of myself. Yes, I am sure some of you are re-reading that sentence more than once. But keep reading I'm going to bless you. Here I am a week in at my parents home, still finding myself having moments where I would spend the whole day in my mom back room crying or in my car so my children would not see me do it so often.

One morning I woke up eyes swollen shut from a long night of crying, walking into the kitchen to fix my coffee so I could sit outside and catch a breeze before my son would wake up. Before I make it to the door my dad is coming through it noticing I had been having one of my episodes, and immediately he grabs me and gives me the biggest hug that a father could have given their child in such a time in need and then his prayer followed behind it this time shouting "Touch her Lord! Touch Her! Meanwhile, I'm standing there screaming in my head asking the devil to "Let me go!" Trusting that my dad prayer had power, I began to sit back and wait to see how soon God was about to move in my life, and when

I tell you he moved expeditiously, until the point that I had no choice but to begin to pray the best way I knew how until the day came that I realized that my prayers could be just as powerful as anyone else prayers. Every morning I woke up I would Thank God, and ask him to break every chain that had me bound, and he did.

My heart is inditing a good matter, I speak of those things which I have made touching the king: my tongue is the pen of the ready writer.

Psalms 45:1

Chapter 9

Break Every Chain

Let me be the first to say, do not be one of those people who believes God only sends what you want, because I will be the first to tell you he does not. Sometimes what we think we want is not what we need, an what we sometimes think we need is not even what we really want. Only God knows best, so trust the process.

"Trust in the lord with all your heart, and do not lean on your own understanding. In all your ways acknowledge him, and he will make straight your paths."

Proverbs 3:5-6

Here I am a month in trying to find my way, still broken, still sad, still hurt, still feeling like dying, still trying to keep the faith, still hoping this man would change, still doubting my strength to be alone, still hoping God would show up, I was just STILL! Meanwhile, God was already setting it up and once everything began to happen, I began to fully understand that having faith is the substance of things hoped for, the evidence of things not seen.

Now, when you learning how God works the struggle of trusting and believing will wear you out if you have no strength to get up and keep fight. Let me share my first fight that I had with the devil. One evening while getting off work tired, busted and disgusted I get in my car, take a deep breath and cranked my car or should I say, "I tried to crank my car." but the key would not turn. So here I am panicking, crying in a dark parking lot by myself not knowing what to do, first thing I did was call my mom screaming telling her my car won't start, meanwhile she is on the other end trying to coach me through it with little to no result at all, finally after trying for a while I tell her to give me a minute to calm down and figure it out. After, sitting there for five minutes in my head feeling numb I realized that I didn't try to call on God for help, but instead I called my mother.

God I need you to show up quickly because I am scared and I do not know what to do! Is the prayer that came out of my mouth before trying to start my car one last time before I listened to the devil in my other ear telling me to call my ex. Guess what!? That last turn of that key in my ignition changed my mind and my life, my car cranked and chills filled my body and I knew then that was God spirit sitting right in that passenger seat the whole time seeing if I was going to pass this test, and I did! Driving home with tears in my eyes thinking what's next God? Before I actually shouted it aloud. Next, morning come I get up and go outside to check and see if it would start and reassure it did not. So, I call on God to show me which way to go. Now I don't know if this was part of the plan but I called my dad who was battling with cancer at the time to tell me what I needed to do in the moment until God showed up, and of course his first question to me was "Have you prayed about it?" Surprisingly to be able to respond with a "Yes!" this time made me feel some type of way because praying had been close to never for years. So, after telling my dad that I had already asked God to show me which way to go, his response was "well then just wait." sitting there lost and confused thinking, what do he mean just wait? I have to be at work, I have to get my kids to school, I have to get back and forth on a daily so what do he mean now wait? I don't have time to wait is what the devil had put in my head. Not realizing God had me in the waiting room for a reason, he was looking down on me seeing if I was using the tools, he had given me from the first prayer I prayed months ago, and I was! Even with the devil still tapping on my shoulders telling me to call my ex for help.

Next morning come, I get up getting ready to drop my car off to the mechanic once we get it started, feeling everything but happy especially since I was not about to have a car for a few days. While waiting on my dad to come follow me to the shop I get a call from my sister who worked for the airport at the time, she had called to tell me she received discounts on rental cars and I can use her discount, so feeling a little at ease from being able to save a little money, I began to realize God was working it out, so I called and made reservations at the rental car place that was literally walking distance from my parents' home, while talking to the guy making the reservations, from driving to the body shop, to riding to the rental lord just make away and he did just that and have not stopped since. What I learned from that moment was all it takes is one simple prayer.

So now that I'm at the car rental place, I walk in signed the papers and follow the salesman outside to show me the car they had for me, which was a 2019 Ford Fusion and when I tell you I feel so in love with this car! I didn't even want to give it back, but I was too scared to go to jail! I found time to do everything I wanted to do just so I could show that car off I felt like I was fit for that car. I start calling my friends telling them "this is going to be my next car!" not realizing or even taking manifesting things seriously because I was just learning God and how he works. But manifesting was exactly what I was doing. So the next morning I get up, get dressed an head to drop my car back off to the rental place, yes you read it correctly "to drop "MY" car off!" Finally, I get my car back out of the shop feeling uncomfortable and anxious for another car, yet trying to stay patient and grateful knowing that God had a plan for me. A few months pass by and I'm ready to trust God and get me a new car, but when fear wants to keep you grounded the anxiety, what ifs, and the I don't deserve it thoughts came tumbling in. One thing about my parents and my God father, is that they always reminded me that I cannot pray and worry, and that was a struggle for me.

So after about 2 months of seeing the rental car I had over and over I began to pray more and more asking God to just reveal what it is that I should do, one thing I began to do while I waited and prayed, I began to Manifest things by being specific in the things that I wanted, got rid of things that became a road block, I asked the universe, I prepared to receive, and practiced Gratitude just like the blog said. So after about a month or so I kept hearing God's voice saying go get it, then the confirmation began to come right after. While dropping my son off at work I see the same exact car that I said was mine at the dealership literally next door but was too afraid to walk in without a dollar in my account. So I continue to go in and order my food at my son job looking out the window at the car picturing me inside of it, then saying a simple prayer in my head still asking God to reveal it, and out of nowhere a flirtatious man walk up to me handing me his business card and offering to buy my food. So because I was broke as a joke at that moment the only thing that distracted me from staring was the fact that I didn't have to slam all the quarters I had in my coin purse on that counter, didn't even think to look at the business card after he handed it to me and given me the invite to come see him. All I wanted was my food. Once I finally get in my car look down at the business card and the gentleman was a car salesman at the dealership next door where the car was parked. With tears in my eyes I backed up out that parking lot and drove home praying and just thanking God for answering my prayer so fiercely, not only did he order my steps into which direction to go, but he feed me and my kids without using my last. Revealing to me he can make a way out of no way. All I could say that night before my eyes closed was "Lord keep making a way!"

Jesus said unto him, I am the way, the truth, and the life, no man come unto the Father except through me.

John 14:6

Chapter 10

Manifest

I'm up early as crap on a Saturday morning doing my hair and make-up preparing myself to go and flirt back with this man from the dealership just so he can bypass the fact that I was making only ten dollars and nine cents a hour, an just put me in the car I've been manifesting about, not thinking for once that God had already approved me, he was just waiting for me to do my part. With no money and the little Faith, I had at the time I walked right in those doors with my face mask on smiling underneath trying to camouflage the fear that I had nudging me on the shoulder forgetting no one could see my smile anyway, let me not forget to mention we were in a pandemic due to covid 19 that was causing complete chaos from deaths, loss of homes, jobs, and being close to your loved ones when we needed them the most. One thing we never lost was God he was here still blessing his children in the midst of all the chaos. So, here I am ready to see what happen with this mustard seed of faith I had, walking up to him, greeting him with a small handshake with him smiling in my face from ear to ear, and instantly turned off just by the fact he didn't have a mask on to protect himself. Hoping this process would be done quickly, I sat in the chair filling out paperwork and getting the job done, finally after four long hours the bank had approved me for my car! When I tell you I didn't know if I wanted to snatch my face mask off and drop to my knees and scream out "Thank You Jesus!" but instead I did it while sitting in my new car I had been manifesting about. What this one situation had taught me after going through my abusive relationship for five years without God in it, is that it is never too late to try God! So I did! And I have not stopped since.

Here I am pulling up to my parents' home, calling my kids on the phone to come out and see their mom in that car they loved just as much as I did. Seeing my kids excited to have something new made me want to do more, so I did! This time I began to do things differently because I saw with my own eyes it works! I just began to manifest and pray, the trusting God part was falling deeply in that circle to, but let me not forget to say it was the hardest thing to do for years but with the help of my family and situations that came along I got it down packed now! Just keep reading I'm going to bless you! I'll never forget waking up that Sunday morning, getting up earlier than usual for work ready to pull up in my new car feeling like a different woman, something I had not felt in years. I walked in to work with all three of my then co-workers screaming "congratulations!" and clapping for me, and that was something I had not gotten in years as well, not because the people around me did not want to clap for me, it was my own self being my own enemy and not even realizing it. Not because I did not want to but, from all the things I was being called from my previous relationships. Like, weak, dumb, lazy, boring, and let's not forget being told nobody would ever want me. Oh! But when I say each day that went by after getting my new car on my own I began to become everything that they said I was not, I became stronger, smarter, motivated, happy, humble, and now an author, last but not least everyone wanted me including him. But all I wanted was God!

Now, here I am manifesting and praying about a new place for me and my children, and a new job that could afford it. I began to wake up daily and Thank God for the things I did not have and asked him to lead me to what he has for me. At the time we were in a pandemic still almost a year in and a delivery service called "Amazon" was in high demand and actually paid decent money or at least more than what I was making at my current job at the beauty supply whose business and hours were slowly decreasing. Meanwhile, I had three kids depending on me so I began to start filling out applications for Amazon warehouse positions and the drivers positions as well just hoping something would happen. Days after doing the applications I continuously began to see Amazon Vans in my mom neighborhood, on commercials, more emails from dsp's for delivery drivers, so I would begin to claim it, smiling while saying out loud "that is my job Jesus and I'm ready whenever you are ready to bless me with it." Days later I received an email from Amazon offering me the position to be a driver making Fifteen dollars and fifty cents which was a lot for me just because I had so little. Not hesitating for a second, I accepted the offer, then ran out of my parents' bedroom I was staying in screaming and crying falling on my knees in the living room filled with joy and disbelief by what God had just did for me.

Meanwhile my dad is sitting on the couch looking at me sideways waiting for me to get it together so he could say "baby I told you all you have to do is give it to God and consider it done!" The crazy part of it all is for once in my life that is all I did. I had been saying and not acting on applying for the position because I always felt like somethings from my past would hinder me and Lord behold all I did was act on it and it happened for me and has not stopped yet.

So, if you have gotten this far in my story, I am quite sure you know what is next for me. Yep! You guessed it, I was out looking for a new place, a place that my kids would love, a safe environment where they could at least go outside to play.

There was this one complex that I had been wanting to move in for years but could never afford it due to my finances, and all of my fears in the back of my mind telling me not to, but now since I began to trust in God more than I had before, things were just happening for me, I started receiving blessings I was not even asking for. But God!

Now, here is the part where I had to learn that God do not always give us what we want, sometimes he gives us what we need, whether that is a job, car, house, friends, and most of all money. For me it was my home, as bad as I wanted to move in this apartment complex that had a big pond full of ducks that baby boy loved so much! God took me back to the same apartment literally that all my trauma was left at and not to mention where I lost him and myself!

Me not knowing until I had done all of the paperwork and paid all of my non-refundable fees and approved over a portal that it was the exact same apartment.

One week before move in I went to go look at the unit to make sure everything was ok. Staying in the same apartments was not the biggest problem, staying in the same exact apartment number where the trauma happened at was.

As the lady turned the leasing cart to the right and parked on the side my stomach tightens and my mouth was watering preparing for the vomit I had sitting at the back of my throat. As we are walking up that sidewalk, I'm hoping this lady did not walk to apartment 1201 and lord behold she did! I did not want to break down and look like a nut case in front of the innocent lady but when I got back in my car I knew I would break or at least I thought I was going to break, the whole ride back to the leasing office instead of questioning God I was asking the devil why and he kept putting those old thoughts back in my head especially after seeing on my move in day my ex-sister in law stayed around the corner in the same complex as well. Feeling confused not knowing if I'm happy to be in my own place again or sad and scared to be reliving everything from my past.

But when God is in the room!!! All I had to do to keep going on, was to just remember God did not bring me this far to leave me now!
Keep Manifesting, Keep Praying.....

For the life was Manifested, and we have seen it, and bear witness, and shew unto you that external life, which was with the father, and manifested unto us.

1John 1:2

Chapter 11

Take My Hands

Now here I go moving in my old place again, but this time just me and my three beautiful children. The only thing different this time is, I have God leading me instead of a man. Whew! Now that was a word all by itself honey. Let me not forget to mention that in the middle of all of my transitioning that God had also sent two people in my life just in the nick of time, well at least that is what I felt. One came in and pulled me away from the harping on being hurt and the trauma I was holding on to, while the other one was teaching me how to put action behind the faith, I said I had. Oh! And the best part about them was they both were Pastors Kids so I trusted the walk with God with them if nothing else! And I knew God had sent them both whether it was for a season, reason, or a lifetime. But in due time I was surely willing to see what it was that God had brewing up.

So let me start with this since this is my true story, they were from the LGBT community and for some reason I felt free enough for once to be me when they came in my life, and that was because they were in a world full of judgement towards them, so for me because I saw them both still standing strong after facing so many things, which let me know in that moment that its possible for me to do the same thing! And not to forget that one holy friend God sent to always remind you that "YOU ARE COVERED!" he knows who he is! Let me just say, I trust God to the max and nobody could ever change that!

My Fears are now gone because I trust that God is going before me. I finally put my fears aside and wrote this book that you are now reading. God sent these two special people to me to push me in a way that they did not even know that they were pushing me to. So, I said all of that to say, God will put it all together before you. He made me wait until I put my trust in him ordering my steps and I did that!

"Trust in the Lord with all your heart, and do not lean on your own understanding. In all your ways acknowledge him, and he will make straight your paths."

Proverbs 3:5-6

So, here I am trying to get comfortable in my new but old place, meanwhile reliving everything that happened there, in the midst of trying hard not to, when walking in each room that reminded me of something I did not want to remember and I decided to just sit, ponder, and stay until it all become a tool to use to get me out of it, I then realize it was all a part of Gods plan for me. Keep reading I am going to bless you!

Each day I woke up I began to just Thank God and ask him to just lead me, because I was willing to follow. I get to work one morning and one of my holy friends bought me some blessing oil from her mom church and told me to go home and anoint my apartment, meanwhile my other friend sending me a song called "Bless my house!" that moment alone I knew we were in synced. My day at work got better because that was confirmation that God was still on this rollercoaster ride with me and was actually the one in control of it the whole time! Thank You Lord! Right now, in this moment as I bless the person reading this. I get home that evening shower, get on my couch and continue to watch my inspirational videos that helped me get through each day. As time went by more things would remind me of why God had placed me back in the same place I had lost him.

Scary as that was for me knowing that God had me alone and the only tool I had to use is what I learned on my way into then, and that was to pray and trust him even when I did not understand.

Each morning I would walk out of my apartment dragging baby boy behind me trying to make sure I did not run into my past that stayed right around the corner if you follow me. But eventually the day that I did was the day that I was actually moving out of the old and into the new. So, with that being said the only thing that I gained in the end of my stay is that God will always protect you from the enemy.

Each day came easier I promise, I woke up and practiced a new prayer each day, I would add something new that I wanted God to do in particular and patiently waited to see his work. This one specific thing I asked on a daily that scared me the most but also taught me that you have to be very careful what you ask for because God is going to deliver it, and that one prayer was "Lord remove anything or anyone in my life that is a distraction in the middle of my transitioning season." and boy oh boy! When I tell you I slowly became disconnected from some family, friends, and some relationships too, but I never stop praying that prayer every night. The one thing that the prayer had taught me along the way was that God was really listening and answering all of my prayers, all I had to do was ask, so I did. And things just start happening for me and my children!

So, here is the part where me and my kids move into the apartment where the ducks lived, after riding pass for almost a whole year and every morning hearing my son screaming at the top of his lungs "Hey Ducks!" God had actually placed us in the apartments in a way that I did not even understand myself. If I did not learn anything in that moment, I learned that not only was prayer the main stream in my life so was manifestation. The biggest part that warmed my heart was that my three-year-old son was the one encouraging me to keep passing by so he can do his morning ritual.

What God was teaching me on this road to greatness is that when he cannot seem to reach me, he will get a hold of the next thing closest to me and that was my children. So, as a single mother I had begun to wise up and gain more knowledge about God and how he works in the universe.

The first thing I began to do, was look at me and my wrongs an nobody else, and that is when my pain turned into peace.

One thing my dad had always instilled in my head was "God is not judging you based on how people treat you, he is judging you based on how you treat people. So, try to do everything with love." and I did! The hardest thing to do sometimes has the biggest blessing waiting on the other side. Just pray and wait.

Each day I began to open up my heart again and let a little love come in, and give a little more too, but the only thing I was not sure I was ready to do was trust that someone else was not going to come in my life and do the same thing to me again. Guess what? With a shattered heart and a new mind, I took that journey.

Do not let what life took you through, stop you from becoming who you were destined to be. My life changed when I let God in. One thing about life you never know how you going to end up living it, you just got to make sure you are taking God with you.

But the lord is faithful, And he will strengthen you and protect you from the evil one.

               Thessalonians 3:3

So, here I am back writing after a long seven month break, and let me just tell you it was well needed so I can give you all the biggest word and advice to take with each and everyone of you. I BEEN THROUGH

HELL AND BACK HERE WRITING TO TELL THE END OF MY STORY! LET'S GO......

These past ten months I was separated from the people I love the most, and depended on the most, not to say that it was for the worst, I will just say God was working it out for my good. I finally found me, and I had to hurt some people along the way, but God knew my heart.

I was putting me and my children first and what made us happy and feel alive. So, I say that to say "You are going to lose some people on the way of finding yourself and your Peace, if they are meant to be they will come back in full force and love every part of the new version of you!" God sent someone in my life who became so patient with me and that is all I needed because lord knows I was not an easy pill to swallow.

All I want to end this story with is LOVE because that is what I found on my journey "Self-Love" you have to learn to love you and I did, the only down side to finding yourself on your journey is that you lose the people you really love along the way, but keep going.

Do It Alone!!

God is going to take all you have to get you there, but what he replaces it with is going to blow your mind.

Last but not least change you, and everything around you to find YOU, because one thing for sure is I finally found ME and I AM HER!!!

LOVE IS

Love is patient, love is kind.
It does not envy, it does not boast,
It is not proud. It does not dishonor
Others, it is not easily angered,
It keeps no record of wrongs.

|

Corinthians 13: 4-5
To Be Continued...........

Made in the USA
Columbia, SC
01 November 2024